ISBN 978-0-332-70091-5
PIBN 11220663

The International Municipal Congress *and* Exposition

Chicago, United States of America
September 18 to 30, 1911

A World Conference *and* Exhibition
for the Development *of* 20th Century
ideals *of* Municipal Economy, Progress
and Perfection.

A Show-Place *and a* Market-Place
for Every Article *of* Material, Machinery
and Equipment that enters into *the*
Construction *and* Operation *of a*
Modern City.

Held with the co-operation *of the*
City *of* Chicago, *the* Chicago Association
of Commerce, *the* Citizen's Association,
the Industrial Club, *the* Civic Federation,
the City Club, *the* United Charities,
and the Rotary Club.

To be held in the Coliseum, the 1st
Regiment Armory and
adjoining plaza.

General Offices: 1107 Great Northern
Building, Chicago, Illinois
Telephones: Harrison 4295; Automatic 64295
Cable Address: "Interexpo, Chicago"

Officially Approved by the United States Government

COPYRIGHT 1908 BY MOFFETT STUDIO CHICAGO

WILLIAM HOWARD TAFT
President of the United States

Who gave the International Municipal Congress and Exposition the endorsement of the United States
Government and engaged to deliver an address before the Congress.

ITY-MAKING is one of the new sciences of the twentieth century. It has been made so by the demand of those who are taxed, that their cities shall be as carefully and economically managed as they themselves manage their business affairs. The result has been that those who govern cities are studying administrative problems more and more searchingly every year.

How can they improve their municipal accounting systems?

How can they raise the standard of their street paving and repair work?

How can they provide more efficient police and fire protection?

How can they draw contracts for public works better to protect their cities from overcharge and from faulty construction?

What do the world's experts say with reference to the best accounting systems for cities to use?

What do the world's foremost thinkers along municipal lines say about city methods?

What is the latest improved machinery that a city can buy to use in its maintenance and growth?

These and many others are the problems that confront the modern city builder.

To solve these questions the **INTERNATIONAL MUNICIPAL CONGRESS and EXPOSITION** was originated.

Two years ago a number of the leaders in the Chicago Association of Commerce first planned to supply, in convenient form, the demand for more general knowledge of the best methods of city government. Never but once in the history of the world had a conference of municipal experts been held, and that was in Berlin many years ago. The attendance was general, but the scope of exhibits was not broad.

It was planned to bring the city officials and students of the development of city life to Chicago to participate in a congress at which free discussion of every subject connected with twentieth century government of cities might be had, to bring out the best ideas of the world's most advanced city experts.

Together with this idea grew a plan to hold, simultaneously with this Congress, an Exposition at which each city so disposed might exhibit features of its administration of which it has reason to be proud, **and at which every up-to-date device for convenience and efficiency in city government might be exhibited by its manufacturers.**

The Chicago Association of Commerce found ready approval of this new project, and many other civic organizations of Chicago agreed to co-operate.

The matter was laid before the City Council and on January 24, 1910, the aldermen voted to co-operate in inviting the cities of the world to participate in the gigantic undertaking. The Coliseum and First Regiment Armory were rented, together with all the available outdoor space adjoining those two structures, and the time for the Congress and Exposition was set to be September 18-30, 1911.

John M. Ewen, who was chairman of the Harbor Commission of the City of Chicago, and consulting engineer in the construction of the new City Hall and County Buildings at Chicago was selected to be chairman of the Congress and Exposition.

Edward H. Allen was made general manager of the Exposition and was given the task of assembling the exhibits that will be shown. He had floor plans of all the exhibit space drawn up and allotted the entire Coliseum annex to the exhibits of the cities, the entire First Regiment Armory to the sessions of the Congress and, in order to pay the enormous expense of the undertaking, arranged to sell the remainder of the floor space for a regular stated price per square foot to the manufacturers of devices and material used by cities.

Curt M. Treat, formerly secretary of the Convention Bureau of The Chicago Association of Commerce, was made secretary of the Congress and Exposition.

John MacVicar, one of the directors of the commission government of Des Moines and formerly mayor of that city, was appointed commissioner-general of the Congress and Exposition and given the task of bearing, in person, invitations to city officials and experts everywhere to join in the deliberations of the Congress and to the city governments themselves to send exhibits to the Exposition. He has toured the United States three times on this mission, with great success. More than six-thousand officials of fifteen-hundred cities of the United States, Canada, and Europe had accepted these invitations up to and including May 15, and at that date, sixty cities had agreed to exhibit.

General offices to transact the complicated business of the great project were opened at 1107 Great Northern building, and a corps of workers assembled, who labor diligently day and night to make the first great International Municipal Congress and Exposition a tremendous success.

The Chicago Association of Commerce early in June sent William Hudson

Harper to Europe to make final arrangements with London, Berlin, Paris and the other principal cities that accepted invitations to send delegates and to exhibit. Before leaving for his tour, the Association of Commerce invited the foreign consuls at Chicago to a luncheon to meet Mr. Harper. They enthusiastically endorsed the Congress and Exposition and each one sent a report on it to his government to pave the way for Mr. Harper's work.

ON April 22d, representatives of The Chicago Association of Commerce went to Washington, D. C., and called on President William Howard Taft and Secretary of State Philander C. Knox. President Taft expressed hearty approval of the International Municipal Congress and Exposition and promised that he would attend the Congress and deliver an address.

Secretary Knox gave his pledge that he would place the influence of the state department behind the Congress and Exposition and instruct the members of the diplomatic and consular staff in every city, with which the United States has diplomatic relations, to vouch for the Congress and Exposition and to urge the officials of these respective cities to send representatives and where possible to send exhibits.

In fulfillment of this pledge Secretary Knox, early in May, sent out the following communication of instruction:

No. 36

DEPARTMENT OF STATE General Instruction Circular

INTERNATIONAL MUNICIPAL CONGRESS AND EXPOSITION AT CHICAGO.

Washington, May 5, 1911.

To the Diplomatic and Consular Officers of the United States.

GENTLEMEN:—

The Department is advised by The Chicago Association of Commerce that there will be held in that city from September 18-30 next an International Municipal Congress and Exposition under the auspices of the Association of Commerce.

This Congress and Exposition will be thoroughly international in its scope, and is the first one of this kind ever held in the United States. It is intended to set forth by municipal experts the advancement of municipalities by showing the possibilities of making city government an asset, and of capitalizing a city's attractions.

It is desired that all cities shall participate in the Congress and Exposition which have anything to offer of advanced ideas along such lines as charters, forms of government, municipal accounting, parks, playgrounds, health, sanitation, charity and correction, taxation, home rule, schools, police, fire and libraries.

It is hoped that each city may be represented by a personal delegation and by some contribution in the shape of models, charts, photographs or views.

Secretary of State PHILANDER C. KNOX

Who placed the stamp of the Official Approval of the United States on the International Municipal Congress and Exposition, by instructing every member of the consular and diplomatic corps to ask the foreign cities to which they were accredited to send delegates and exhibits.

The presence of experts of world-wide fame and known ability will make possible at this Congress comparisons between communities and cities, thus offering to some the opportunity of contributing, and to others the privilege of learning.

Formal invitations will be, at a later date, forwarded by the Chicago Association of Commerce directly to the municipalities.

There will be held at the same time, in Chicago, an International Good Roads Congress.

While these Congresses are not under the auspices or official patronage of the Government of the United States, this Government would be glad if the Government of the country to which you are accredited would give due publicity to the Congresses mentioned and would recommend the sending of delegates to those Congresses by the municipalties and organizations which may be interested.

Two copies of the prospectus of the International Municipal Congress and Exposition are enclosed.

You will communicate to the Foreign Office the invitations to the Congresses, and request that due publicity may be given to them.

I am, Gentlemen,   Your obedient servant,

P. C. KNOX.

Early in May, general manager Allen addressed a letter to Mayor Carter H. Harrison of Chicago, advising him of the action that had been taken by the city council preceding his administration, at which time the council indorsed the project, and asking that arrangements be begun for a pretentious exhibit to be shown by the city of Chicago.

At a meeting of the city council Mayor Harrison laid this subject before the aldermen, and upon the recommendation of the finance committee, a sub-committee of aldermen was appointed to prepare Chicago's exhibit and $5,000 was appropriated to cover the expense. Alderman Richert, chairman of the city council finance committee, was made chairman of this exhibit committee, and those named as his associates were Aldermen Harding, Block, Tearney, and Sitts. These men got into communication at once with general manager Allen, and began arrangements of the city to exhibit its harbor plans, its city playground system, and several other features of Chicago's government.

Prominent among the cities that are preparing exhibits are New York, which is planning to show its famous budget exhibit; Boston; Philadelphia; Washington, D. C., which will display the uniform municipal accounting system devised for it by Le Grand Powers; Cincinnati, which will show models of the Queen & Crescent railroad, said to be the only municipally owned steam railroad in existence; Toledo; Detroit; St. Louis; New Orleans; Minneapolis, which will exhibit the labor-saving devices used in building and maintaining all its public works by day labor; St. Paul; Kansas City, which will display its municipally operated road building machinery; Denver, with its street lighting and reclamation of city waste land; Seattle; Spokane; Portland, Ore., and the California cities, which will co-operate in an extensive exhibit under the management of the California League of Municipalities.

When the exposition feature was laid before the larger business men of the United States who deal in the lines of manufacture of machinery for cities, they at once saw the wonderful possibilities of the undertaking. The biggest and most substantial corporations of this country at once made early selections of space and it became assured that this department would not only be of the greatest educational interest, but also of vast commercial significance.

Following the notification the cities had received and the personal and informal invitations urged upon them by Commissioner General MacVicar, The Chicago Association of Commerce sent to every city in the world, of 5,000 or more population, a beautifully engraved invitation to take part in the Congress and Exposition. The return mail brought acceptances in great numbers and succeeding mails brought names of officially appointed delegates.

Action of the cities was almost unanimous in instructing delegates to examine with particular care all of the commercial exhibits shown at the Exposition; to compare the respective merits of different makes of machinery and material and to make note of comparative prices. In other words, the delegates to the Congress will throng the Exposition as authorized purchasing agents, inspecting the exhibits with a view to finding out what to buy for their cities.

The city of Des Moines went further than this and more than a year prior to the Congress and Exposition instructed its heads of departments to make no more contracts for the purchase of machinery or supplies until the holding of the Exposition and to be prepared to make contracts for the purchase upon the floor of the Exposition by Des Moines of whatever it needed.

New York appointed twenty-seven delegates, one or more from each department of its city government, to listen and contribute to the discussions of the Congress and to inspect the exhibits of the Exposition.

Other cities hastened to appoint delegates representing their several departments and the mail of the first two days after these appointments began to arrive at the general offices, brought the names and official positions of more than three hundred officially appointed delegates. The work of preparing credentials for these was begun at once and committees of leading citizens were appointed to aid in their entertainment while here and to facilitate their work of examination of the exhibits and participation in the Congress.

THE making up of a program to guide the Congress in its deliberations, was begun in the summer of 1910 by Commissioner General MacVicar and officials of the Chicago Association of Commerce. This monumental task will not have been completed much before September first. The classification of subjects is so wide as to embrace every problem, major or minor, that any city official has to grapple with in the performance of his duties. Speakers of world wide reputation as city experts have been invited to contribute to the conference. Men highly specialized in particular branches of municipal research have been asked to co-operate and have promised to do so. Among the speakers early engaged after the completion of the first parts of the program of subjects were the following:

William Howard Taft, President of the United States.

Right Honorable James Bryce, Ambassador Extraordinary and Plenipotentiary to the United States from Great Britain.

Carter H. Harrison, Mayor of Chicago.

Darius A. Brown, Mayor of Kansas City, Mo., and President of the League of American Municipalities.

John E. Reyburn, Mayor of Philadelphia.

John F. Fitzgerald, Mayor of Boston.

Emil Seidel, Mayor of Milwaukee.

Geo. W. Perkins of New York.

Frederick A. Cleveland, Chairman of the United States Economy and Efficiency Commission at Washington, D. C.

Andrew Rinker, City Engineer of Minneapolis, Minn.

Jas. C. Trevilla, Superintendent of Streets of St. Louis.

Ella Flagg Young, Superintendent of Schools of Chicago.

James G. Berryhill of Des Moines, Ia.

Secretary Childs of the Short Ballot System.

Dr. LeGrand Powers, Head of the Government Statistical Bureau at Washington, D. C.

William A. Prendergast, Comptroller of New York City.

Consulting Engineer Tillston of Manhattan, New York.

James M. Head, Ex-Mayor of Nashville, Tenn.

E. B. DeGroot of the Playground Association of Chicago.

Sherman Kingsley, Superintendent of the Chicago Associated Charities.

Edward F. Croker, Ex-Fire Chief of New York City.

F. A. Kohler, "Golden Rule" Police Chief of Cleveland, Ohio.

Chas. C. Healey, Captain of the Chicago Mounted Police.

Dr. Geo. W. Kohler of Rochester, N. Y.

Dr. Wm. A. Evans, Former Health Commissioner of Chicago.

Milo R. Maltby, Public Service Commissioner of New York City.

Bion J. Arnold, Chairman and Chief Engineer of the Board of Supervising Engineers, controlling Chicago's traction problems.

George W. B. Hicks, City Planning Expert of Philadelphia, Pa.

Harvey S. Chase, Director of the "Boston 1915 Movement."

Henry E. Legler, Librarian of the Chicago Public Library.

Allen Ripley Foote, President International Tax Association and President Ohio State Board of Commerce, Columbus, Ohio.

Lawson Purdy, Commissioner Taxes and Assessments, New York City.

J. W. Harris, Assessment Commissioner, Winnipeg, Man.

Chas. E. Merriam, Former Head of the Merriam Commission of Chicago.

FIRE fighting apparatus and material will be among the most important and the most interesting exhibits at the Exposition. The fire chiefs of the principal cities of the United States and Canada will meet at the annual Convention of the International Association of Fire Engineers at Milwaukee, Wis. during the first two or three days of the Congress and Exposition. The chiefs have been invited to become the guests of the Congress and Exposition at the expiration of their Convention and a lake steamer has been chartered to bring them to Chicago in a body. They will take part in the deliberations of the Congrees on fire protection and kindred subjects and then inspect the exhibits of fire fighting supplies on the floor of the Exposition.

For the first time in history the fire chiefs will not have merely to examine the apparatus exhibited and then take back to the city officials who have purchasing power, reports as from former exhibitions of fire apparatus, but they will have the city officials who possess the right to purchase, with them on the floor of the Exposition and will direct the attention of these to the respective merits and prices of various kinds of apparatus and material.

The state fire marshals of the United States and the marshals of the provinces of Canada also will be guests of the Municipal Congress and Exposition. These are members of the Association of State Fire Marshals of North America. These met in convention at the Hotel LaSalle in Chicago, Thursday, June 15th. On that date General Manager Allen appeared before them and offered a formal invitation to the members of that organization to join the fire chiefs of the cities as guests of the Congress and Exposition.

Among the delegates to the Congress in addition to those sent by the cities will be delegates at large or general representatives of foreign countries. Japan, for instance, will send several representatives to study city methods of every nation with a view to profiting thereby, if possible, in the administration of Japanese cities.

Not the least important of the delegates to the Congress will be those sent by civic and commercial organizations in the various cities. Formal invitations have been sent to all such organizations to send representatives to co-operate with the delegates of the cities.

GOOD roads will be another of the most important subjects before the Congress and will be illustrated by exhibits at the Exposition. Already manufacturers of paving materials and machinery have contracted for space in large numbers to show their products. The National Good Roads Association, foreseeing the great importance of these exhibits, decided to take advantage of them and arranged to hold the Fourth Annual International Good Roads Congress conjointly with the International Municipal Congress and Exposition.

Voting devices will have important places among the exhibits and their discussion will receive a great deal of attention at the Congress. Many election officials are numbered among the officially appointed delegates. Voting machines of many makes will be exhibited in the north end of the balcony of the Coliseum and complicated voting contests that will test the efficiency of these machines to the utmost, will be arranged so that every visitor to the Exposition will be able to vote on each device, thus trying out the rapidity and accuracy with which automatic voting may be done.

WATER service for cities is perhaps the most vital single subject that confronts city officials with absorbing problems. There is more money spent by municipalities in the establishment and maintenance of water works than almost any other public utility. Therefore, water supply with all the kindred subjects that relate to it will absorb a great deal of the attention of the city delegates and others who join in the deliberations of the Congress. Especial attention will be shown also to the exhibits that have to do with supplying residents of cities with water.

To this end a special invitation has been sent to the officials of the American Water Works Association to co-operate with the management of the Congress and Exposition by sending delegates to the Congress and by helping with suggestions and in other ways to secure comprehensive and authoritative discussion of water problems.

The importance of the Exposition department is comprehended at once when it is contemplated that delegates to the Congress after a discussion in the Congress Hall of, for instance, the respective merits of motor driven and horse drawn fire apparatus, will at once step out on to the floor of the Exposition in the same building and examine the exhibits as illustrative of the arguments and addresses just heard.

JOHN M. EWEN, Chairman   CURT M. TREAT, Secretary

JOHN MacVICAR, Commissioner General

EDWARD H. ALLEN, General Manager of Exposition

===== GENERAL OFFICES =====

1107 GREAT NORTHERN BUILDING
CHICAGO

Telephones: Cable Address:
HARRISON 4295   **"INTEREXPO,**
AUTOMATIC 64295   **CHICAGO"**

CHICAGO PLAN DRAWING

View Looking North on the South Branch of the Chicago River, Showing the Suggested Arrangement of Streets and
Ways for Teaming and Reception of Freight by Boat at Different Levels.

From a painting for the Commercial Club by Jules Guerin.
Used by courtesy of the Commercial Club.

The History of an Old Bank

THIS Bank was incorporated by S. W. Rawson and his associates as the Union Trust Company in 1869. It has been located at the corner of Dearborn and Madison Streets since its organization, except for the period immediately after the Great Fire, and is one of the four oldest banking institutions in Chicago. The officers in charge of the bank have been associated with it for years. Mr. S. W. Rawson was its president until his son, Frederick H. Rawson, was elected to that office, in which capacity the latter has since served this institution.

Mr. F. L. Wilk and Mr. G. M. Wilson, two of the vice-presidents, have been with the bank since its incorporation, and have had a large share in shaping the bank's policy during the last forty years. To assist in taking care of its rapidly increasing business Mr. H. A. Wheeler, formerly president of the Credit Clearing House, well known to the business men of Chicago, was added to the staff during the first part of 1910. Mr. F. P. Schreiber, the cashier, has been associated with the bank for forty years.

Beginning with the modest capital of $125,000, which was all the capital actually paid in, this bank has steadily progressed, maintaining its integrity during all those years when the tendency towards consolidation among Chicago banks was so strong. Its policy has always been to apply the greatest part of the profits to the building of reserve against deposits. By this process it has increased its capital and surplus account from the original $125,000 to $2,350,000 at which it now stands, every dollar of which increase has been made through sound, conservative banking methods.

In the period from 1901 to 1911 the deposits of the Union Trust Company have increased from $4,883,686 to $16,470,562, showing a steady, healthy growth of business with the public.

The officers of this bank have always maintained a public spirited interest in civic affairs and we have taken this space to show this interest in a concrete way. We invite delegates to this convention to call and make themselves at home at the bank.

TRIBUNE BUILDING
Madison and Dearborn Streets

Delegates to Congress

This list is necessarily incomplete. Many cities have not yet appointed delegates.

NEW YORK CITY—27

Dr. John W. Brannan, President. Bellevue and Allied Hospitals.

J. Gabriel Britt, President, Board of Elections.

Charles Strauss, President, Board of Water Supply.

David Fergusen, Supervisor, Board of City Record.

Kingsley L. Martin, Commissioner, Department of Bridges.

Patrick A. Whitney, Commissioner, Board of Corrections.

Calvin Tomkins, Commissioner, Department of Docks and Ferries.

Egerton L. Winthrop, President, Board of Education.

William A. Prendergast, Comptroller, Department of Finance.

Dr. Ernst J. Lederle, Commissioner of Health.

Charles B. Stover, Commissioner of Parks, Manhattan and Richmond.

Michael J. Kennedy, Commissioner of Parks, Brooklyn and Queens.

Thomas J. Higgins, Commissioner of Parks, Bronx.

George H. Chatfield, Secretary, Permanent Census Board.

Michael J. Drummond, Commissioner, Department of Public Charities.

William H. Edwards, Commissioner, Department of Street Cleaning.

Lawson Purdy, President. Department of Taxes and Assessment.

Henry S. Thompson, Commissioner. Department of Water Supply, Gas and Electricity.

Joseph Johnson, Commissioner, Fire Department.

Rhinelander Waldo, Commissioner, Police Department.

William R. Willcox, President, Public Service Commission.

John J. Murphy, Commissioner, Tenement House Department.

Cyrus C. Miller, President, Borough of Bronx.

Alfred E. Steers, President, Borough of Brooklyn.

George McAneny, President, Borough of Manhattan.

Lawrence Gresser, President, Borough of Queens.

George Cromwell, President, Borough of Richmond.

BOSTON, MASSACHUSETTS—28

John F. Fitzgerald, Mayor.

Walter L. Collins, President City Council.

John T. Priest, City Clerk.

Thomas Allen, Chairman Art Commission.

Richard M. Walsh, Chairman Bath Commission.

Frederic H. Fay, Bridge Commissioner.

Arthur G. Everett, Building Commissioner.

Dr. Charles P. Putnam, Chairman Children's Institutions Department.

John A. Mullen, Fire Chief.

Dr. Samuel H. Durgin, Chairman Board of Health.

Horace G. Wadlin, Librarian.

Robert S. Peabody, Park Commissioner.

Fred S. Gore, Commissioner Penal Institutions.

Stephen O'Meara, Police Commissioner.

William J. Casey, Superintendent Printing Department.

Louis K. Rourke, Commissioner Public Works.

James H. Sullivan, Highway Division Engineer.

Frank A. McInnes, Sewer and Waterworks Division Engineer.

Joseph H. Caldwell, Superintendent Water Rates.

Edward A. Wade, Supervisor Lighting Service.

David A. Ellis, Chairman School Committee.

Salem D. Charles, Street Commissioner.

Frank O. Whitney, Chief Engineer.

J. Edward Mullen, Superintendent of Supply Department.

Charles B. Woolley, City Sealer.

James E. Cole, Commissioner Department.

PITTSBURG, PENNSYLVANIA—9

William A. Magee, Mayor.

Joseph G. Armstrong, Director Department of Public Works.

John M. Morin, Director Department of Public Safety.

Dr. E. R. Walters, Director Department of Public Health.

A. C. Gumbert, Director Department of Charities.

E. S. Morrow, City Controller.

Adolph Edlis, City Treasurer.

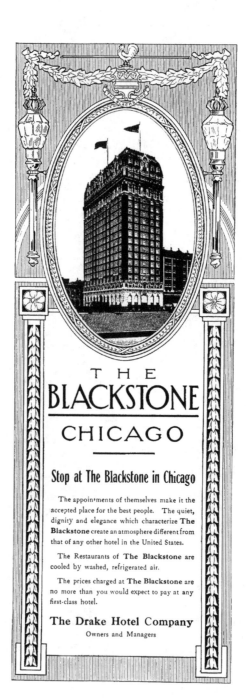

CHARLES A. O'BRIEN, City Solicitor.
THOS. J. HAWKINS, Chief Assessor.

BUFFALO, NEW YORK—8

LOUIS P. FUHRMANN, Mayor.
WILLIAM G. JUSTICE, Comptroller.
CLARK H. HAMMOND, Corporation Counsel.
NEIL McEACHREN, Treasurer.
HENRY P. EMERSON, Superintendent of Education.
FRANCIS G. WARD, Commissioner of Public Works.
LOUIS J. KENNGOTT, Overseer of the Poor.
WILLIAM P. BRENNAN, Chief Judge City Court.

BALTIMORE, MARYLAND—15

JAMES H. PRESTON, Mayor.
FRANK N. HOEN, Architectural Commissioner.
EDGAR ALLAN POE, City Solicitor.
HARRY F. HOOPER, Comptroller.
BENJAMIN T. FENDALL, City Engineer.
EDWARD M. PARRISH, Fire Commissioner.
ALFRED M. QUICK, Water Engineer.
O. F. LACKY, Harbor Engineer.
JOSEPH L. WICKES, Commissioner Street Cleaning
CALVIN W. HENDRICK, Chief Engineer Sewerage Commission.
SHERLOCK SWANN, Police Commissioner.
EDWARD D. PRESTON, Inspector of Buildings.
JOHN E. SEMMES, School Commissioner.
JAMES H. VAN SICKLE, Superintendent of Schools.
W. W. CHERRY, President City Council.
DR. JAMES BOSLEY, Commissioner of Health.

OMAHA, NEBRASKA—16

JAMES C. DAHLMAN, Mayor.
LOUIS BURMESTER, President City Council.
DAN B. BUTLER, City Clerk.
FRANK A. FURAY, City Treasurer.
C. O. LOBECK, Comptroller.
HARRY E. BURNAM, City Attorney.
CHARLES H. WITHNELL, Building Inspector.
GEORGE W. CRAIG, City Engineer.
THOMAS J. FLYNN, Street Commissioner.
RALPH W. CONNELL, Health Commissioner.
WALDEMAR MICHAELSEN, City Electrician.
JOHN C. LYNCH, Plumbing Inspector.
JOSEPH SCULLY, Milk Inspector.
CHARLES F. CROWLEY, Gas Commissioner.

ROBERT U. WOLFE, Boiler Inspector.
JOHN G. PEGG, Inspector Weights and Measures.

MINNEAPOLIS, MINNESOTA—15

JAMES C. HAYNES, Mayor.
ARTHUR W. SELOVER, President City Council.
C. A. BLOOMQUIST, City Treasurer.
DAN C. BROWN, City Comptroller.
HENRY N. KNOTT, City Clerk.
DANIEL FISH, City Attorney.
G. L. FORT, City Assessor.
ANDREW RINKER, City Engineer.
C. W. RINGER, Chief Engineer, Fire Department.
MICHAEL MEALEY, Superintendent of Police.
DR. P. M. HALL, Commissioner of Health.
JAMES G. HOUGHTON, Inspector of Buildings.
A. D. MEEDS, Inspector of Gas.
W. R. YOUNG, Registrar Waterworks.
E. T. SYKES, Supervisor Waterworks.

ST. PAUL, MINNESOTA—6

H. P. KELLER, Mayor.
C. H. O'NEILL, Corporation Attorney.
WM. H. FARNAM, Comptroller.
S. A. FARNSWORTH, City Treasurer.
O. CLAUSSEN, Commissioner of Public Works.
GEO. T. REDINGTON, City Clerk.

NEW ORLEANS, LOUISIANA—7

MARTIN BEHRMAN, Mayor.
CHARLES R. KENNEDY, Comptroller.
OTTO F. BRIEDE, Treasurer.
GEORGE S. SMITH, Commissioner of Public Works.
ALEX PUJOL, Commissioner of Public Buildings.
I. D. MOORE, City Attorney.
WILLIAM J. HARDEE, City Engineer.

DETROIT, MICHIGAN—17

PHILIP BREITMEYER, Mayor.
CHARLES A. NICHOLS, City Clerk.
P. J. M. HALLY, Corporation Counsel.
DAVID E. HEINEMAN, City Comptroller.
MAX C. KOCH, City Treasurer.
JACOB J. HARRER, Commissioner.
R. H. McCORMICK, City Engineer.
JOSEPH H. RUMNEY, Superintendent Garbage Collection Department.

The Congress Hotel and Annex

Formerly Known as the Auditorium Annex

Located on Michigan Boulevard — Chicago's most aristocratic thoroughfare—overlooking Grant Park *and* the broad expanse *of* beautiful Lake Michigan ✕ ✕ Two minutes from the city's activities ✕ ✕ ✕ ✕

RATES: Rooms, one person, bath detached, $2.00 and up; with private bath $3.50 and up
Rooms, two persons, bath detached, $3.00 and up; with private bath $5.00 and up
SUITES—Prices on Application

N. M. KAUFMAN, President.

Adv. No. 1

MAX L. TEICH, CARL C. ROESSLER, Managing Directors.

HOTEL CONGRESS ANNEX

FRANK ALDRICH, Superintendent Street Cleaning.

FRANK H. CROUL, Commissioner.

MYRTLE P. HURLBUT, Commissioner Department Parks and Boulevards.

JAMES C. BRODERICK, Chief Water Supply Department.

GEORGE B. SHEEHY, President Public Lighting System.

FREDERICK J. CLIPPERT, President Waterworks System.

WILLIAM B. STRATTON, President Department of Buildings.

DR. CHAS. F. KUHN, President Board of Education.

W. C. MARTINDALE, Superintendent of Schools.

INDIANAPOLIS, INDIANA—12

SAMUEL LEWIS SHANK, Mayor.

EDWARD A. RAMSEY, City Clerk.

HARRY R. WALLACE, City Comptroller.

JOSEPH B. KEALING, Corporation Counsel.

MERLE N. A. WALKER, City Attorney.

MARTIN J. HYLAND, Superintendent of Police.

CHARLES E. COOTS, Chief of Fire Department.

HENRY W. KLAUSMANN, City Civil Engineer.

JOSEPH L. HOGUE, Superintendent of Streets.

WILLIAM L. RESONER, Chief Inspector of Sweeping and Sprinkling.

THOMAS A. WINTERROWD, Building Inspector.

ISADOR WULFSON, Inspector of Scales, Weights and Measures.

NASHVILLE, TENNESSEE—17

HILARY E. HOWSE, Mayor.

G. W. STAINBACK, Chairman Board of Public Works.

W. W. SOUTHGATE, City Engineer.

HENRY CURRAN, Chief of Police.

A. A. ROZETTA, Chief of Fire Department.

GEORGE RYER, Superintendent Waterworks.

PATRICK CLEARY, Superintendent of Streets.

S. F. MOSBY, Superintendent Sprinkling and Workhouse Keeper.

J. T. BEAZLEY, Superintendent Scavenger Department.

W. E. DANLEY, Inspector of Meters.

LYLE ANDREWS, Comptroller.

CHAS. MYERSM, Treasurer.

HENRY SCHARDT, Sealer of Weights and Measures.

DR. W. E. McCAMPBELL, Chairman Board of Health.

E. E. BARTHELL, Chairman Board of Education.

J. J. KEYES, Superintendent of Public Schools.

F. P. McWHIRTER, Chairman Board of Park Commissioners.

GALVESTON, TEXAS—6

LEWIS FISHER, Mayor.

J. H. KEMPNER, Commissioner Finance and Revenue.

H. C. LANGE, Waterworks and Sewerage Commissioner.

A. P. NORMAN, Police and Fire Commissioner.

V. E. AUSTIN, Commissioner Streets and Public Property.

JOHN D. KELLEY, City Secretary.

DENVER, COLORADO—4

ROBERT W. SPEER, Mayor.

JOHN CONLON, President Board of Aldermen.

DR. W. M. ROBERTSON, President Board of Supervisors.

HENRY READ, President Board of Public Works.

CLEVELAND, OHIO—9

HERMAN C. BAEHR, Mayor.

HENRY F. WALKER, President of Council.

NEWTON D. BAKER, City Solicitor.

HILAND B. WRIGHT, City Auditor.

HARRY L. DAVIS, City Treasurer.

A. B. LEE, Director of Public Service.

F. G. HOGAN, Director of Public Safety.

G. M. DAHL, Street Railway Commission.

R. Y. McCRAY, City Clerk.

PORTLAND, OREGON—13

A. G. RUSHLIGHT, Mayor.

HENRY A. BELDING, President of the Council.

JAMES W. MORRIS, City Engineer.

DAVID C. CAMPBELL, Chief of Fire Department.

ARTHUR M. COX, Chief of Police.

ALEX DONALDSON, Superintendent of Streets.

WILLIAM HEY, Inspector of Plumbing.

H. E. PLUMMER, Building Inspector.

DR. C. H. WHEELER, Health Officer.

E. T. MISCHE, Parkkeeper.

FRANK T. DODGE, Superintendent of Water Department.

HARRY N. NAPIER, Superintendent of Garbage Crematory.

F. G. BUCHTEL, Sealer of Weights and Measures.

GRAND RAPIDS, MICHIGAN—4

JAMES SCHRIVER, City Clerk.
Aldermen:

Invitation

to the

Municipal and Highway Officials

who propose to attend the

International Municipal

Exposition

During the past thirty years, practically every city of importance and most counties and towns in the country have purchased road making or street cleaning machinery from The Austin-Western Company, Ltd. of Chicago. Since our home city has been selected as the meeting place for the first International Municipal Congress, we feel that we should have the privilege of showing some attention to the municipal and highway officials who visit Chicago at that time.

So that adequate provision may be made, it is important that those who expect to attend should notify us by filling out and mailing to us the below coupon as early as possible.

In addition to having a booth on the main floor of the Coliseum we will give daily a moving picture exhibition of modern road making and street cleaning machinery in operation under various conditions in different sections of the country. This is a much more impressive and effective way of comparing the methods in use for this work at different points. We will also be prepared to take delegates through our plants, the largest Factories devoted exclusively to the manufacture of road and street machinery in the world and demonstrate any of the following. Street Sprinklers, Street Sweepers, Gasoline Road Rollers, Gasoline Mowers, Road Graders and Levelers of all sizes, Elevating Graders and Wagon Loaders, Rock Crushers both gyratory and jaw type, Dump and Spreading Wagons and Wheelers, Drags and plows.

Make your headquarters at our offices at 910 S. MICHIGAN BLVD. only a few blocks from the Coliseum where the exposition is to be held.

————CUT HERE————

THE AUSTIN-WESTERN CO., LTD., CHICAGO

I expect to attend the International Municipal Exposition in Chicago and will reach there about

My address while in Chicago will be, _____

_____ *Name* _____ *Title*

Address _____

JOSEPH RANIHAN.
G. C. OSWALD.
WILLIAM DeBOER.

LITTLE ROCK, ARKANSAS—17

CHAS. E. TAYLOR, Mayor.
FRED HOLDER, Alderman.
H. C. McCAIN, Alderman.
J. H. TUOHEY, Alderman.
JOHN RIEGLER, Alderman.
C. E. SMITH, Alderman.
WM. L. ROGOSKI, Alderman.
J. H. HOLLIS, Alderman.
L. N. WHITCOMB, Alderman.
CHRIS. LEDWIDGE, Alderman.
WM. LANGE, Alderman.
C. F. CUNINGHAM, Alderman.
LOUIS VOLMER, Alderman.
GEO. A. STRATMAN, Alderman.
J. A. ADAMS, Alderman.
GEO. W. PARDEE, Alderman.
H. A. PITTARD, Alderman.

TOLEDO, OHIO—6

BRAND WHITLOCK, Mayor.
J. R. COWELL, Director Public Service.
J. J. MOONEY, Director Public Safety.
CORNELL SCHREIBER, City Solicitor.
J. J. LYNCH, City Auditor.
C. M. FEILBACH, City Treasurer.

DALLAS, TEXAS—9

W. M. HOLLAND, Mayor.
J. HOWARD ARDREY, Pres. Dallas Planning League.
J. ELMER SCOTT, Pres. Playgrounds Ass'n.
J. J. SIMMONS, Mgr. Boren-Stewart Co.
JOHN W. PHILIP, a Director of Dallas Ad. League.
M. H. MAHANNA, c/o Dexter & Mahanna, Ins.
GEO. B. DEALEY, Mgr. Dallas Morning News.
EDWIN J. KIEST, President Times-Herald.
J. O. ANDERSON, Manager Dallas Dispatch.

JOLIET, ILLINOIS—8

EDWARD M. ALLEN, Mayor.
JESSE R. BROCKMAN, Alderman.
GEORGE WOODRUFF, Banker.
WM. H. CLARE, Broker.
BERNARD L. KELLY, Alderman.

THOMAS DORORAN, Lawyer.
M. HARNEY, Alderman.
FRANK E. HEWETT, Manager Rate Association.

ROCKFORD, ILLINOIS—27

W. W. BENNETT, Mayor.
E. A. WETTERGREN, City Clerk.
EDWIN MAIN, City Engineer.
CARTER H. PAGE, JR., Superintendent of Water Works.
DR. W. E. PARK, Commissioner of Health.
A. E. BARGREN, Chief of Police.
T. E. THOMAS, Fire Chief.
NICHOLAS NOLAN, City Sealer.

ALDERMEN.

GUST PETERSON,
JOHN A. HALLDEN,
EDWIN P. BARRETT,
OSCAR H. OGREN,
E. A. ANDERSON,
WM. STENLUND,
F. J. LEONARD,
JAMES T. JOSLIN,
MARK T. STOREN,
WM. F. WARNER,
EMMET F. WILSON,
ERNST E. SMITH,
WM. W. DICKINSON,
JOSEPH SULLIVAN,
CHARLES ANDREWS, JR.

FIRE AND POLICE COMMISSIONERS.

FRED E. CARPENTER, President.
CHARLES MALM,
C. H. C. BURLINGAME,
C. C. LOFQUIST, Secretary.

SAULT STE. MARIE, MICHIGAN—2

A. J. SHORT, Mayor.
F. T. McDONALD, City Attorney.

GRINNELL, IOWA—7

J. H. PATTON, Mayor.
J. W. GANNAWAY, Chairman, Streets and Alleys.
F. S. EDGE, Chairman, Sewers.
A. McBLAIN, Chairman, Water.
A. C. HARRIMAN, City Clerk.
H. L. BEYER, City Solicitor.
C. E. HARRIS, Health Physician.

THE First National Bank of Chicago was organized forty-eight years ago, in 1863, and since that time its growth has been coincident with that of the City of Chicago and the vast area which is commercially tributary thereto. The Capital in 1863 was $205,000, to-day its capital and surplus is $20,000,000. In 1863 the first published statement showed deposits of $273,000; they now exceed $116,000,000. The First National was the eighth institution to receive the approval of the Comptroller of the Currency. To-day there are more than seven thousand national banks in the association.

With the growth of the National Bank came the demand for trust and savings facilities, met in 1903 by the organization of the First Trust and Savings Bank, with a capital stock of $1,000,000. The stock of this bank is owned by the stockholders of the First National Bank. The growth has been marked. In less than eight years its capital and surplus has reached $5,500,000 with more than $52,000,000 in deposits. The growth of the bond and trust departments has been equally great. The former offers for sale only such securities as have been purchased primarily for the bank's own investment; while the latter acts as trustee, administrator and in other fiduciary capacities, both for individuals and corporations, under the authority of the law.

The First National Bank of Chicago, the First Trust and Savings Bank and the National Safe Deposit Company, located in the First National Bank Building at the northwest corner of Dearborn and Monroe streets, cordially invite those interested in the International Municipal Congress to visit their offices.

JAMES B. FORGAN,
President.

C. E. Bolling, City Engineer.
E. E. Davis, Superintendent of Water Works.
W. P. Knowles, Superintendent of Gas Works.
O. A. Hawkins, Commissioner of Revenue.
James B. Pace, City Treasurer.
Benjamin T. August, City Clerk.

INDEPENDENCE, MISSOURI—3
Llewellyn Jones, Mayor.
James S. Craig, City Clerk.
H. H. Pendleton, City Engineer.

GREENVILLE MISSOURI—5
Wm. Yerger, Mayor.
J. M. Robertshaw, Councilman.
A. V. Wineman, Councilman.
A. J. Cannon, Councilman.
Lyne Starling, City Clerk.

AMERICUS, GEORGIA—8
J. E. Mathis, Mayor.
C. J. White, Secretary, Board of Trade.
Frank Sheffield, Chairman, County Commissioners.
J. B. Ansley, City Engineer.
L. G. Council, Chairman, Street Commission.
Robert Christian, Superintendent of Roads, Sumter County.
Dr. J. W. Chambliss, Chairman, Board of Health.
A. G. Miller, Superintendent, Public Schools.

BROWNSVILLE, TEXAS—1
Benjamin Kowalski, Mayor.

WILMINGTON, NORTH CAROLINA—1
Thomas D. Meares, City Clerk.

ELGIN, ILLINOIS—1
Albert Fehrman.

MT. HOLLY, NEW JERSEY—1
William H. Mason, Chairman of Governing Committee.

MATTOON, ILLINOIS—4
E. T. Guthrie, Mayor.
C. L. James, City Engineer.
F. A. Heermans, City Clerk.
Ira Powell, City Attorney.

ANNISTON, ALABAMA—1
J. L Wikle, Mayor.

WINCHESTER, MASSACHUSETTS—1
Preston Pond, Selectman.

ANDERSON, SOUTH CAROLINA—4
J. L. Sherard, Mayor.
C. E. Tally, Alderman.
G. C. Sullivan, City Attorney.
C. M. McClure, Alderman.

BOULDER, COLORADO—1
Dr. John B. Phillips, Alderman.

FERGUS FALLS, MINNESOTA—8
A. G. Anderson, Mayor.
Chas. D. Wright, President First National Bank.
Elmer E. Adams, Editor "Journal."
D. M. Brown, Ex-Mayor.
Dr. O. T. Sherping, Member Board of Health.
D. A. Tennant, Fergus Flour Mills.
N. F. Field, City Attorney.
Leonard Eriksson, Attorney.

MOBERLY, MISSOURI—1
Willard P. Cove, Mayor.

GULFPORT, MISSISSIPPI—5
J. W. Thomas, Mayor.
N. D. Goodwin, City Clerk.
Aldermen:
M. P. Bouslog,
G. J. Baltz,
S. R. Sueed.

BOONE, IOWA—4
John S. Crooks, Mayor.
B. P. Holst, Councilman.
William Crowe, Councilman.
F. L. Gorppenger, Councilman.

AMARILLO, TEXAS—2
J. H. Patton, Mayor.
E. T. Miller, City Attorney.

FRANKFORT, KENTUCKY—8
James H. Polsgrove, Mayor.
E. H. Taylor, Jr., Ex-Mayor of Frankfort.
W. P. D. Haly, Ex-Adjutant General of Kentucky.
J. C. W. Beckham, Ex-Governor of Kentucky.
L. F. Johnson, Attorney at Law.

J. H. Hazelrigg, President Civic League.
W. G. Sirripson, Mayor Pro Tem. Frankfort.
W. S. Farmer, Chairman Executive Committee, Business Men's Club.

MARSHALL, TEXAS—3
T. S. Caven, Mayor.
E. J. Fry.
H. B. Pitts.

HARRISBURG, ILLINOIS—5
J. B. Blackman, Mayor.
J. M. Pruett.
Herman Martin.
J. W. Shaw.
Thos. Davenport.

SELMA, ALABAMA—1
J. L. Clay, Mayor.

ATLANTA, GEORGIA—1
Courtland S. Winn, Mayor.

DOWAGIAC, MICHIGAN—2
D. C. Thickstun, Mayor.
Wm. T. Easton, City Clerk.

DULUTH, MINNESOTA—2
M. B. Cullum, Mayor.
Joseph Shurtel, President of the Council.

WICHITA, KANSAS—5
J. H. Graham, Mayor.
E. T. Battin, Commissioner.
H. J. Roetzel, Commissioner.
R. B. Campbell, Commissioner.
E. M. Leach, Commissioner.

DU QUOIN, ILLINOIS—1
E. E. Jacobs, Mayor.

SIOUX CITY, IOWA—3
A. A. Smith, Mayor.
R. S. Whitley, Superintendent Public Safety Councilman.
Geo. M. Kellog, Chief of Fire Department.

ROCK ISLAND, ILLINOIS—5
H. M. Schriver, Mayor.

M. T. Rudgren, Commissioner, Department of Accounts and Finance.
Archie Hart, Commissioner, Department of Health and Safety.
Robert R. Reynolds, Commissioner, Department of Streets and Public Improvements.
Jonas Bear, Commissioner, Department of Public Property.

TERRE HAUTE, INDIANA—2
Louis Gerhardt, Mayor.
Levi G. Hughes, City Comptroller.

CHILLICOTHE, OHIO—4
Wallace D. Yaple, Mayor.
Walter W. Boulger, Clerk of Council.
James A. Cahill, Vice-Mayor.
Claude B. Schaeffer, City Solicitor.

MAYWOOD, ILLINOIS—14
Ode L. Rankin, Mayor.
T. Fred Laramie, Attorney.
Albert W. Holden, Treasurer.
Charles W. Strook, Collector.
Frank W. Wickman, Superintendent Waterworks.
Samuel H. Donaldson, Clerk.
Louis Sweeney, Chief of Police.
D. C. Everitt, Trustee.
W. H. Scott, Trustee.
L. J. McGinnis, Trustee.
B. F. Oakes, Trustee.
H. W. Page, Trustee.
J. Burdick, Trustee.
Emory R. Hayhurst, Physician.

MIDDLETOWN, NEW YORK—1
Rosslyn M. Cox, Mayor.

CLINTON, ILLINOIS—5
Geo. S. Edmonson, Mayor.
Frank Rundle, Department of Accounts and Finance.
J. F. Moffett, Department of Streets and Public Improvement.
Charles L. Dickinson, Department of Public Property.
James M. Kirk, Department of Public Health and Safety.

City Exhibits

At the date of publication of this prospectus the list of exhibits to be sent to the exposition by the cities was not completed. The cities that had been allotted space were as follows:

New York City—New York's famous budget exhibit; docks and ferries; sanitation methods.

Chicago—Subway plans; harbor plans; official Chicago plan; school methods; library methods; health department methods; playgrounds.

Philadelphia—Parks; widening of streets; comprehensive street planning.

Boston—Public baths; playgrounds; street improvements; city planning.

Rochester—Public health; city planning.

United States Bureau of Commerce and Labor—Uniform municipal accounts and reports.

Washington, D. C.—City planning.

Des Moines—Street construction; civic center; commission government; moving pictures of municipal undertakings.

St. Louis—City planning; city improvements.

Milwaukee—Municipal dance halls and theatres.

Pittsburg—Traction investigations, comparing street car facilities in the United States with those in Europe.

Denver—Artistic streets; street lighting; reclamation of waste city property.

Baltimore—New $20,000,000 sewer system, showing sewer construction and disposal by sceptic tanks, shown by models and drawings; municipal subways; conduits for wiring.

Columbus—Best organized municipal electric lighting plan in the United States; extensive system of water filtration; collection and reduction of garbage.

Kansas City—Road building; playgrounds.

St. Paul—City planning.

Minneapolis—Public construction by day labor.

San Francisco—Civic center; feature development plans.

Cleveland—New civic center.

Portland—Parks.

New Haven—Improvement commission.

Seattle—City planning.

Buffalo—Grade crossing improvements; water works; docks and markets; city planning.

Port Sunlight, England—Drawings and Photographs of this, said to be the ideal industrial city.

Hartford—City planning.

Detroit—Parks and boulevards.

Toledo—Parks and boulevards.

Dayton—City planning.

Liverpool, England—Docks.

Hamburg, Germany—City planning.

Cologne, Germany—City planning.

Amsterdam, Holland—City planning.

Subjects for Congress

Among the classifications of topics for discussion at the Congress are the following:

CHARTERS AND FORMS OF GOVERNMENT

The consideration of the various forms of commission and other systems of municipal government.

Non-partisan elections for city government.

Combining of legislative and executive functions and tax-levying and tax-spending powers in one small body.

Short ballot.

Abolishing ward lines and electing at large.

MUNICIPAL ACCOUNTING

Modern methods of municipal bookkeeping.

Reports and publicity giving comparisons one year with another and making possible comparisons one city with another.

Budget making.

PAVING AND CARE OF STREETS

Street paving. Material and manner of construction.

Paving repairs and municipal asphalt plant.

Street cleaning, showing modern equipment and organization best adapted.

Street lighting, artistic modern methods adapted to cities and towns.

ROAD MAKING

Macadam and bituminous macadam.

Oiled roads and methods of caring for natural surface roadways.

Improved machinery for modern road making.

PARKS AND PLAYGROUNDS

Care and beautification of parks and boulevards.

Improved equipment for children's playgrounds.

Public baths.

HEALTH AND SANITATION

Sewers and sewage disposal plants.

Prevention and suppression of epidemics.

Garbage collection.

TAXATION

Equalizing taxation.

Restriction of city's taxing powers.

Method of collecting taxes.

Special assessment tax.

Personal property tax.

CHARITIES AND CORRECTIONS

Almshouses.

City work houses and reformatories.

Prevention of crime.

HOME RULE

Restriction of city's powers of self-government by state legislature.

Restriction on indebtedness of cities.

PUBLIC UTILITIES

Control of public service companies by city and state.

Indeterminate franchise.

Municipal ownership.

Street lighting.

Water systems.

Docks and water transportation.

Meters—high pressure.

Modern housing.

CITY PLANNING

Making cities attractive and wholesome.

Landscape architecture and public buildings.

Civic centers and boulevards.

Tree planting and preservation.

CIVIC ORGANIZATIONS

Real assistance to a city government.

Scope of their work.

COMMERCIAL ORGANIZATIONS

Things every citizen should know about his city.

Relations to municipal government.

SCHOOLS

Building on scientific principles.

Public care of children. Medical inspection.

Health more important than education.

Successful methods of teaching.

Kindergartens and day nurseries.

Public playgrounds.

POLICE AND FIRE

Police and police courts.

Juvenile courts and the probation system.

Preventing and fighting fires.

Preventing crime rather than making criminals.

Criminal identification systems.

LIBRARIES—MUNICIPAL STATISTICS

How a library can assist a city government.

General Exhibits

Among the many articles for city use, the following will be shown at the exposition.

Adding and listing machines
Ambulances
Antiseptics
Antitoxin
Ash handling systems
Asphalt paving
Auto fire engines
Auto fire patrols
Auto police patrols
Auto street sprinklers
Auto sweepers
Auto trucks
Automatic fire doors
Automatic fire windows
Automatic sprinklers
Auxiliary fire equipment

Ballbearing hinges
Bascule bridges
Bitulithic paving
Bituminous macadam pavements
Bituminous concrete pavement
Brick-facing
Brick-paving
Bridge building
Building construction machinery
Building material for municipal construction

Card index systems
Cement garbage boxes
Cement paving
Centrifugal sewage pumps
Church equipment
City surveying materials
Chemicals
Clay products
Concrete drains
Concrete mixers
Concrete sidewalks
Concrete spreaders
Concrete supplies
Condensers
Creosoted wood block paving
Criminal identification systems

Deodorizers
Desks
Disinfectants
Drainage and curbing
Drainage systems
Draughting supplies
Dredging and ditching machines
Drinking fountains

Educational exhibits, including every school necessity
Electric apparatus
Electric locomotives
Electric meters
Electric motors
Electric sanitary appliances
Elevators
Envelope sealing machines

Fire alarm stations
Fire and burglar proof vaults
Fire boats
Fire doors
Fire engines

Fire engine houses
Fire engine house equipment
Fire escapes
Fire extinguishers
Fire houses
Fire windows
Firemen's uniforms
Fireproofing apparatus
Formaldehyde
Formalin
Flexible metal hose
Flood gates
Fly swatters
Fly screens

Garbage disposal systems
Garbage wagons
Gas meters
Gas testing machines
Grade curbing
Grain elevator transmission and equipment

Harness
Heating systems for schools
Hod elevators
Hoisting engines
Hose carriages
Hose carts
Hospital appurtenances
Hospital furniture

Impervious wall facing
Incinerating stations
Inspection bureaus

Laboratory supplies
Lamp posts, city lighting appliances and lamp globes, reflectors, etc.
Lighting fixtures

Macadam pavements
Machinery for city infirmaries, including laundry machinery
Metal culverts
Metal lath
Motors, generators, converters
Motorcycles
Municipal office appliances
Municipal office furniture

Office supplies used in municipal accounting
Office furniture
Ornamental bridges
Ornamental iron works
Ornamental lamp posts

Paving and road making devices
Playground models
Police flashlight systems
Police patrol wagons
Police uniforms
Power and pump house conduits
Prism plate glass
Prism system for daylighting buildings
Prison equipment

Reinforced concrete
Road grading apparatus
Road oiling machines
Road rollers

Roofing
Rubber lined cotton fire hose and couplings
Rural municipal plows

Sand and clay pumps
Sand blast for iron work
Sanitary devices for public buildings
Sanitary garbage disposal plants
Sanitary garbage wagons
Sanitary street cleaners
Scales
School seating
School books and supplies
Septic tanks
Sewer pipe
Sewage pumping stations
Sewerage disposal plants
Sewerage systems
Sewer cleaning devices
Sidewalk construction
Sidewalk doors
Sightseeing autos
Sludge valves
Smoke stacks
Steam road rollers
Steam shovels
Steel ceilings
Steel forms for culverts and bridges
Steel rails
Stone road construction
Street brooms
Street car lighting
Street cars
Street flushers
Street lighting systems
Street sprinklers
Street sweepers
Structural ornamental steel
Supplies for libraries, schools, hospitals, jails, court rooms
Surface railroad frogs

Tabulating machines
Technical schools
Telautographs
Telephones
Testing laboratories
Tile
Trade schools appurtenances
Transportation devices
Trees

Uniforms

Vaccine
Vacuum cleaning equipment
Vacuum cleaning machinery
Vacuum cleaners
Ventilating systems
Ventilators, jail cells, prison construction
Vitrified brick
Vitrified pipe
Voting machines

Wagons—garbage and waste
Wagons—dump
Water meters
Wood paving

Railway Terminals

The railway passenger stations, with their locations and the railroads using each are as follows:

CENTRAL STATION—Park row and 12th street; south side.

Chicago, Cincinnati & Louisville.

Cleveland, Cincinnati, Chicago & St. Louis (Big Four).

Illinois Central.

Michigan Central.

West Michigan.

Wisconsin Central.

CHICAGO & NORTHWESTERN—West Madison and Canal streets, west side; All divisions.

DEARBORN STATION—Dearborn and Polk streets; south side.

Atchison, Topeka & Santa Fe.

Chicago & Western Indiana.

Chicago, Indianapolis & Louisville (Monon).

Erie.

Grand Trunk.

Wabash.

GRAND CENTRAL STATION—Fifth avenue and Harrison street; south side.

Baltimore & Ohio.

Chicago Great Western.

Chicago Terminal Transfer.

Pere Marquette.

LASALLE STREET STATION—Van Buren and LaSalle streets; south side.

Chicago & Eastern Illinois.

Chicago, Rock Island & Pacific.

Lackawanna.

Lake Shore & Michigan Southern.

New York, Chicago & St. Louis (Nickel Plate).

UNION STATION—Canal street, between Adams and Madison; west side.

Chicago & Alton.

Chicago, Burlington & Quincy.

Chicago, Milwaukee & St. Paul.

Pittsburg, Fort Wayne & Chicago.

Pittsburg, Cincinnati, Chicago & St. Louis (Pan Handle).

Local Transportation

The main entrance to the Congress and Exposition will be the front door of the Coliseum. This is in Wabash avenue near 15th street.

Cottage Grove avenue trolley line stops at the door. The cars may be boarded at any point in Wabash avenue downtown or in Cottage Grove avenue on the south side.

Indiana avenue trolley line stops at the door. These cars also run in Wabash avenue downtown and on the south side run in Indiana avenue.

All east and west car lines on the south side, from 18th street south, transfer to the Cottage Grove and Indiana avenue lines.

The State street trolley line runs one block west of the Coliseum. It may be taken in State street either downtown or south.

The Wentworth avenue line runs three blocks west of the Coliseum and may be taken in Clark street downtown or in Wentworth avenue south.

The Halsted street line also runs in Clark street, three blocks west of Wabash avenue.

From the north side, the through-route cars in Clark street stop three blocks west of the Coliseum.

From the west side, the 12th street cars connect with the Cottage Grove avenue and Indiana avenue cars at Wabash avenue.

The South Side Elevated trains may be taken at any station on the union loop downtown. There is a station at 12th street, three blocks north of the Coliseum. Coming from the south side, there is a station at 18th street, three blocks south of the Coliseum.

HOTEL PLANTERS

WILL OPEN ABOUT AUGUST 1st
1911

Clark and Madison Streets, CHICAGO, ILL.

EUROPEAN PLAN   TOM JONES, Manager

RATES:

Without Bath
$1.50 to $2.00

Two in Room
$2.50 to $3.50

FIRE PROOF

HOTEL PLANTERS RESTAURANT

*This is the most elegant Restaurant in Chicago.
It is cooled by a refrigerating system so you can
enjoy a meal in the hottest weather.
The Elegance in finish, the Artistic Mural Dec-
orations of Francois I, the Splendor of ceilings,
walls and costly furnishings, create the most
agreeable surprise.*

THE SERVICE IS THE BEST
MODERATE PRICES

RATES:

With Bath
$2.00 to $3.50

Two in Room
$3.00 to $4.50

NEW and MODERN

A HOME for COMMERCIAL MEN in the HEART of CHICAGO

Hotels

There are several hundred hotels in Chicago, but the following is a list vouched for by the International Municipal Congress and Exposition, from any of which delegates may reach the Coliseum by a street car in from five to twenty minutes:

Auditorium Hotel, 216 Michigan ave.

Blackstone Hotel, Michigan ave. and Hubbard Place.

Brevoort Hotel, 143 Madison st.

Congress Hotel and Annex, Michigan ave. and Congress st.

Great Northern Hotel, Jackson boul'v'd and Dearborn st.

Kaiserhof Hotel, 266 Clark st.

Hotel Majestic, 22 Quincy st.

Hotel Sherman, 56 Clark st.

Hotel Vickery, 1204 Wabash ave.

Hotel Victoria, Clark and Van Buren streets.

La Salle Hotel, 120 La Salle st.

Lexington Hotel, 2135 Michigan ave.

New Southern Hotel, Michigan ave. and 13th st.

Palmer House, State st., cor. Monroe.

Planters Hotel, Clark and Madison streets

More Commercial Clubs, Improvement Associations and Municipalities have used the advertising columns of The Inter Ocean *in the last ten years than have used the advertising columns of all other Chicago newspapers put together.   :   :   :*

Chicago Examiner

THE TWENTIETH CENTURY NEWSPAPER

An advocate of better Municipal Government; business methods in the management of municipalities; a forward movement to give to the people in public improvements the value they pay in taxes; a closer harmony between municipalities, working for the general public welfare, The Examiner extends to the delegates to the

International Municipal Congress

a hearty welcome. The Examiner is proud of its place as a humble worker in the ranks of the progressive institutions of America and believes great good will come from the Congress of the Municipalities of the world.

Chicago Headquarters Waterman's Ideal Fountain Pen

In the noted city of Ober-Ammergau there was perhaps only one instance during the recent production of biblical stories that would carry one's thought back to the City of Chicago.

The large and notable audience of tourists from every part of the world would, for hours, be quietly and interestingly absorbed in the details of the wonderful production, the unique surrounding and the pleasures of the climate, which permitted the sky to become the roof of so picturesque a setting.

With all this uniqueness, there was one custom which, owing to its prevalence among almost the entirety of this cosmopolitan assemblage, impressed one most forcibly at the close of the play. The audience would rise and practically deluge the many places where the attractive Post Cards of this picturesque country were for sale, and it was a strange sight to see hundreds of people before leaving for their respective points, standing around the scene of the Passion Play and addressing these cards to every point of the universe.

The exclusive and necessary use of fountain pens could not help but cause one to reflect on the magnificent headquarters of the L. E. Waterman Company, on Clark street, Chicago, which is one of the places visited by almost every tourist of that locality before leaving on a tour.

We learn that Waterman's Ideal Fountain Pens are purchased from dealers in every city, town and hamlet, in every country, on the face of the earth, and that these branch stores, similar to the magnificent headquarters in Chicago, are maintained for the purpose not only to distribute to the retail stores of their section, but for attention which may be required by individual users, and which attention the dealer, who sold the pen, has in most cases neither the facilities nor the time to extend. It is for this reason that the branch stores of the L. E. Waterman Company assist in the repairs and exchanges of tourist's pens as a surety of the most complete satisfaction in the use of their pens, when most needed, that is, during travels when other methods of writing are inaccessible or inconvenient.

The Chicago Store of the L. E. Waterman Company is centrally located on Clark street, between Adams and Monroe streets, in the neighborhood of the Ticket Offices of Steamship and Railroad Lines. The interior is entirely finished off in mahogany, with inlaid paneling, quite similar to the general style of the interior of a Pullman car. The walls and ceiling are beautifully designed and tinted and the entire effect is as fine or finer than that which we have ever seen in any store of the kind. The vaults and stock-rooms quite resemble those of a banking office, which, we learn, is due to the fact that great care is necessary in the carrying of thousands of dollars worth of this well-known pen. A regular banking system is in force in the handling, checking and balancing of the stock. There are fifty feet of show-case display space in the store, affording an excellent opportunity for those interested to look over the entire line, and at these cases, which are comfortably arranged with seats, one may remain and try the various styles of Waterman's Ideal Fountain Pens until entirely suited, when the pen points or entire pens may be exchanged to the complete satisfaction of the owner. There is a very comfortable little room partitioned off on one side of the main store, where one may enjoy the writing comforts of the most modern hotel. The marvelous advance of the usefulness of this small but important factor of business and social life today has developed a wonderful business.

New York is the home of the L. E. Waterman Company, where is located President F. D. Waterman, who has managed the development of the Company so thoroughly and completely in advance of the actual requirements, and in accordance with his optimistic ideas, that this Company today is so well organized in every part of the world that the great traveling public cannot help but thoroughly appreciate the superiority of Waterman's Ideals and the care, thought and attention that may be received at every branch of their business.

The Fountain Pen has come to stay, and, supplied under the familiar name "Waterman's Ideal," has proven to be one of the most useful mercantile articles of the present age.

Building the Western Country
In Wonderful Completeness

To make a country with its cities, villages, highways, railroads, forests, orchards and farms of every sort in the space of a few years would seem to be a work of fancy only.

H. L. Hollister & Co. will make a demonstration at the coming International Municipal Exposition that will surprise those who have not kept pace with the reclamation of the desert.

The Kuhn organization of which H. L. Hollister & Co. are a part is in the midst of the greatest work of empire building now going on, involving the expenditure of many millions of dollars. They have placed thousands of families upon the wonderful irrigated farms of the Idaho and California deserts.

The lands have been redeemed by irrigation and the people have been invited to come and make their homes under ideal conditions.

Accompanying this annoucement is a copy of one of their advertisements such as they are using in the press throughout the United States.

Low values are put upon the land and thousands of fortunes have been made and still are being made by those who are sharing in this development.

It is very interesting to know about this work of reclaiming and developing hundreds of thousands of acres and also very profitable for those who take part in it.

The irrigated farm is the ideal farm because crops are always sure. No irrigating farmer would think of returning to farming under humid conditions.

Successful farmers must have cities, towns and railroads. All this sort of development has been carried on together and makes an important chapter in the country's history.

H. L. Hollister & Co. are always glad to give a little time to anyone who wants to talk about getting a home or farm in Southern Idaho or the Sacramento Valley of California, or who wants to join in this interesting work of development of desert lands.

AN EXTENSIVE EXHIBIT OF IRRIGATED PRODUCTS IS MAINTAINED AT 35 WEST MONROE STREET, IN THE NATIONAL CITY BANK BUILDING, WHICH EVERY ONE IS INVITED TO SEE

General offices of H. L. HOLLISTER & CO.
1101 Home Insurance Bldg., 137 S. La Salle Street,   -   -   -   CHICAGO, ILL.

Queen of Havana Cigars

CORINA

JOSE ESCALANTE & CO.

The Cigar of Cigars

La Azora

HABANA

Lilienfeld Bros and Co.

CHICAGO, ILLS.

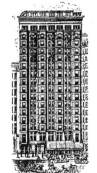